I0816110

BEATRICE AND THE NIGHTINGALE

Patricia Newman

Illustrations by

Isabelle Follath

Margaret Quinlin Books

PEACHTREE

ATLANTA

Published by Margaret Quinlin Books
An imprint of PEACHTREE PUBLISHING COMPANY INC.
1700 Chattahoochee Avenue
Atlanta, Georgia 30318-2112
PeachtreeBooks.com

Text © 2026 by Patricia Newman
Illustrations © 2026 by Isabelle Follath

All rights reserved. No part of this book may be reproduced, transmitted, or stored in an information retrieval system in any form or by any means, graphic, electronic, or mechanical, including photocopying, taping, and recording, without prior written permission from the publisher. Additionally, no part of this book may be used or reproduced in any manner for the purpose of training artificial intelligence technologies or systems, nor for text and data mining.

Edited by Margaret Quinlin and Vicky Holifield
Design and composition by Jennifer Browne

The illustrations were created with ink and watercolor.
Printed and bound in October 2025 at C&C Offset, Shenzhen, China.
1 3 5 7 9 10 8 6 4 2
First Edition
ISBN: 978-1-68263-727-2

Cataloging-in-Publication Data is available from the Library of Congress.

EU Authorized Representative: HackettFlynn Ltd, 36 Cloch Choirneal,
Balrothery, Co. Dublin, K32 C942, Ireland. EU@walkerpublishinggroup.com

For Erowyn Beatrice —P.N.

To my sister —I.F.

No one knew Beatrice would make history.

Born in India, she was simply Colonel John and Annie Harrison's curly-haired second daughter. Her proud parents nicknamed her Baba.

Music surrounded Baba and her family and followed them from India to England.

Flute as silvery as the wind.

Singing as merry as birdsong.

Violin as lively as a butterfly.

The “tello” was too big for Baba, but she could learn the basics of music. Mother started her with the five-finger exercises every piano player learns.

Soon, Baba also began violin lessons to train her fingers for the cello.

What joy when two more sisters joined the Harrison family!

May, Beatrice, Monica, and even one-year-old Margaret played violin concerts. They made magic that brought people together.

Baba's heart sang.

One day Mother came home with a cello in her arms.

The glossiest wood!

The purest voice!

Finally Baba could play cello. She dreamed of sharing its music with the world.

One short year later, Baba played for Sir George Martin, an examiner for the Royal College of Music.

Her cello sang like a nightingale.

"My child, someday I think the musical world will hear of you and your cello," he said.

His words fed the dream in Baba's heart.

She practiced and practiced until her fingers ached.

Then the Harrisons moved to Germany, the music capital of the world. Beatrice studied and practiced while her pet canaries sang.

She perfected her tone.
She flourished her bow.
She learned to say "I will" rather than "I cannot," and her fingers flew along the strings.

Music filled Beatrice with joy, a gift she shared with all who listened.

At seventeen she won the biggest music prize in all of Germany. She was the youngest competitor ever—and the first cellist—to win.

Back in England, Beatrice acquired a special cello nearly two hundred years old.

The cello of her dreams,
the color of the setting sun.

She called it Pietro.

Beatrice and Pietro shared their music with fans in European concert halls, with royalty, and with the President of the United States. Audiences stood as one to shower them with bouquets.

At one concert in Russia, the audience applauded through twenty-seven encores! The adoring fans then carried Beatrice out of the hall on their shoulders. They removed the horses and pulled her carriage through the streets themselves.

Beatrice and Pietro shared music wherever they went.

When war broke out, they soothed injured soldiers and lifted the spirits of their beloved nation.

After the war, they traveled from city to country and back again.

Until one day . . .

At home in the English countryside, Beatrice played her best-loved melodies in a garden of blue flowers to her chirping pet birds and the rabbits and shrews of the woods.

When she stopped, a nightingale's voice echoed her cello. Beatrice trilled up and down the strings. The voice of the bird followed. The more Beatrice played, the more the nightingale sang.

She had never heard birdsong like this before. "A miracle!"

Night after night Beatrice played Pietro, and the nightingale sang along. But why should Beatrice be the only one to hear them perform together?

She had an idea . . .

The next day Beatrice played a concert aired by England's new radio company. Why, she wondered, couldn't it broadcast her duet with the nightingale? She told the boss, Sir John Reith, about her idea.

"Wild goose chase!" he blustered.

"Waste of time!" he exclaimed.

"Impossible!" he protested.

Beatrice knew the nightingale might soon find a mate and leave. It was now or never.

She explained how Sir John could change the world with the first live outdoor broadcast, the first wild bird broadcast from nature.

A miracle of the modern age!

Finally, he agreed to Beatrice's wish.

On a spring night in 1924, radio engineers placed a microphone in a thicket of oak leaves and connected it to amplifiers stacked in the summerhouse. The amplifiers sent a signal through the Harrisons' telephone line to the radio station.

The engineers stood by, ready to begin broadcasting the moment the nightingale started singing.

Beatrice played Pietro for almost two hours.
Rabbits gnawed the wires.
Insects buzzed.
Squirrels chittered.
The Harrisons' donkey brayed.
But the shy nightingale remained silent.
Beatrice and the engineers nearly gave up.

Suddenly the nightingale burst into song, his trills loud and sweet!

He followed Pietro's mellow sound and added his own flair to a melody that would surely attract a mate.

Listeners around the world heard the duet. Some with outdoor radios said their nightingales sang too. Others listened to a friend's radio by telephone. In places like Scandinavia and Scotland, where nightingales never nest, listeners heard the beautiful song for the first time.

A million people marveled at music, nature, and science in harmony.

Every spring for the next twelve years, when nightingales returned to Beatrice's garden to find mates, they sang with her cello.

And for twelve years the radio shared their duets worldwide.

Beatrice invited listeners to her garden.

They came by the hundreds from Canada and Japan, from Australia and the U.S., from gardening clubs and nature clubs.

And then a glorious chance meeting at a recording studio became one of the greatest moments of Beatrice's life.

The King of England interrupted her session, and before she could curtsy, he said: "Nightingale, nightingale, you have done what I have not yet been able to do. You have encircled the Empire with the song of the nightingale with your cello."

Beatrice's heart sang.
Her dream had come true.

NOTABLE MOMENTS IN BEATRICE'S LIFE

1892—Beatrice Harrison is born in India on December 9.

1893—The Harrisons return to England with baby Beatrice and her older sister May.

1894—Beatrice attends her first concert, and the cello captivates her.

Circa 1895—Beatrice begins piano lessons.

Circa 1896—Beatrice begins learning violin.

1897–1899—Beatrice's sisters Monica and Margaret are born.

1901—Beatrice receives her first cello.

1903—Beatrice and May enter the Royal College of Music in London.

1907—Beatrice makes her debut as a cellist at Queen's Hall.

1910—At age seventeen, Beatrice is the first woman, the first cellist, and the youngest competitor to win the Mendelssohn Prize.

1911—Beatrice acquires Pietro, and they tour the concert halls of Europe.

1913—Beatrice plays at the White House for President Wilson.

1916—Beatrice plays for injured soldiers at British Red Cross concerts.

1922—The Harrisons move to Foyle Riding in Surrey, England.

1924—The nightingale sings with Beatrice and Pietro in the BBC's first live broadcast of the duet.

1925–1936—The duets continue and Beatrice hosts thousands of visitors in her garden.

1937—Beatrice leaves Foyle Riding.

1937–1941—After Beatrice leaves Foyle Riding, the BBC continues to record nightingales singing alone.

1945–1965—Beatrice continues to give concerts until her last appearance in 1958. She lives quietly with her sisters until her death in 1965.

A nightingale singing for a mate. T Harbig / Alamy

THE STAR PERFORMER

Nightingales used to be found all over the United Kingdom, but are now endangered because of climate change and habitat loss.

Nightingales have brown backs, rusty tails, and white breasts. They seek out bushes near the ground rather than treetops and love scrubby, wooded habitats where they can hide. Their song, however, is anything but shy. Males use whistles, trills, rattles, and warbles to woo potential mates. Their songs are considered the most beautiful in the bird world. In 1924, most people had never heard them sing.

You can listen to a nightingale here: https://macaulaylibrary.org/asset/23656

BEATRICE'S PIETRO

Beatrice's cello "Pietro" was made in 1739 by Pietro Guarneri of the Republic of Venice in what is now Italy. It is one of only five or six cellos made by Guarneri, and collectors say its brilliant voice makes it the best of the bunch.

A rich American patron lent Beatrice some money to buy this rare cello. And Princess Victoria, the favorite sister of King George V, repaid the debt for her dear friend Beatrice.

Beatrice's Pietro, made in 1739 by Pietro Guarneri. Harrison cello photographs courtesy of David L. Fulton.

The cello is a member of the violin family of instruments, but it is larger and makes lower-pitched sounds. To produce the low notes, craftsmen experimented by increasing the size of the instrument and the length of its strings. It worked, but the instrument could no longer be held in the musician's arms! Craftsmen solved this problem by adding a stand to rest on the floor when the cello was played.

BIRTH OF RADIO

Radio might seem old-fashioned in our era of streaming music and video, but it was the world's first spoken communication over a distance. More than one hundred years of science contributed bits and pieces to the discovery of radio. In 1820, Hans Christian Oersted from Denmark discovered that a magnetic field is created around a wire that has electricity running through it.

BBC engineers prepare the microphone to capture the nightingale's song. Look and Learn

In 1864, James Clerk Maxwell of England found that these electromagnetic currents travel at the speed of light. Then Italian inventor Guglielmo Marconi shocked the world when he telegraphed the results of the America's Cup yacht races from a ship at sea to a land-based station in New York.

Radio as we know it was born in 1906 when Reginald Fessenden of Canada sent the first long-distance transmission of the human voice. Demand for radios exploded. Millions of people wanted to hear news, music, comedies, variety shows, and game shows in their own homes.

The BBC broadcast its first program in 1922. Two short years later it broadcast Beatrice, her cello, and the nightingale performing together. Beatrice and her nightingales performed annually in her garden for the next twelve years.

To learn more about radio, visit this website: https://www.youtube.com/watch?v=t2pvQY1u_2Q

A HOAX?

In a 2022 BBC podcast, a bird expert said the BBC arranged to have a professional bird mimic standing by in case Beatrice's nightingale refused to perform that May 19th night in 1924. He claimed the bird did not sing and the bird mimic filled in. He closed the podcast with a recording of the "fake" nightingale singing as Beatrice plays her cello.

But Patricia Cleveland-Peck, the editor of Beatrice's autobiography, has found no evidence of a May 19, 1924, recording or that a bird mimic was present. In a May 2022 article, she states that Beatrice's sister Margaret and a man hired to lay cables both told her they were in the garden with Beatrice and that they never saw a bird mimic. In addition, Cleveland-Peck says, "I cannot believe that [the] founding father of the BBC, John Reith, would have countenanced such a deception." And she cannot imagine that Beatrice could have been fooled so completely. "Beatrice with her musician's ear and her familiarity with the nightingales in her garden would sure[ly] have noticed something different about the bird's song."

Beatrice wrote these words in her diary: "The broadcasting experiment was repeated . . . the following week and arrangements were made to install two microphones the following year." So, like Cleveland-Peck, we have to wonder, "If the original broadcast was such a nerve-wracking fiasco, why was the . . . BBC willing to repeat it the following week?"

Such is the nature of writing nonfiction: Sometimes researchers have to choose which evidence is most plausible and convincing. After all the research that went into the preparation for *Beatrice and the Nightingale*, I agree with Cleveland-Peck that the broadcast of the nightingale singing with Beatrice and her cello was genuine.

Beatrice Harrison and one of her many dogs in Surrey, 1925. Lebrecht Music & Arts / Alamy

You can listen to a May 3, 1927, recording of Beatrice with a real nightingale here: https://www.youtube.com/watch?v=IU1Z7QtyJVs

A NOTE FROM THE AUTHOR

I first heard about Beatrice's story while watching a movie called *The Dig*, about a famous archaeological site in England. In one scene, a young archaeologist and a Royal Airforce pilot chat about nightingales. The archaeologist remarks that she had only heard a nightingale over the wireless. She goes on to tell the pilot about Beatrice Harrison, a famous cellist who convinced the BBC in 1924 to broadcast a nightingale singing as she practiced cello in her garden. The pilot had never heard of Beatrice—and neither had I. So, I began my own dig.

In 1924, when Beatrice and the BBC first shared the nightingale's song over the airwaves, people usually visited concert halls to celebrate the beauty of music together. Streaming services and earbuds didn't exist. Even radio was new. On top of all that, no bird had ever before been broadcast live from nature. A new, more sensitive microphone that could pick up sounds and convert them to electromagnetic waves made this crazy idea possible. Listeners were shocked because the sounds were so close to those in nature.

Beatrice remembers that night of May 19, 1924, in her autobiography:

> *At about nine o'clock I crept up with my cello to a ditch and placed my chair half in and half out of it quite crooked, but I knew that the exquisite voice was there, under a thicket of oak leaves, ready to sing to his little wife. . . . I shall never forget his voice that night, or his trills, nor the way he followed the cello so blissfully. It was a miracle to have caught his song and to know that it was going, with the cello, to the ends of the earth.*

I love this meeting of music, nature, and science. I hope you do as well and will enjoy digging into Beatrice's miraculous story as much as I did.

Patricia Newman

SELECTED BIBLIOGRAPHY

BBC. "Beatrice Harrison, cello and nightingale duet." *History of the BBC*. Accessed May 6, 2021. https://www.bbc.com/historyofthebbc/anniversaries/may/cello-and-nightingale-duet.

Berkeley, Michael, host. *Private Passions*. "Tim Birkhead." BBC Radio 3, April 17, 2022. Podcast. https://www.bbc.co.uk/programmes/m001691s.

Cleveland-Peck, Patricia, ed. *The Cello and the Nightingales: The Autobiography of Beatrice Harrison*. John Murray, 1985.

Cleveland-Peck, Patricia. "Defending the Duet: The Cello and the Nightingale." *The Strad*, May 11, 2022. https://www.thestrad.com/playinghub/defending-the-duet-the-cello-and-the-nightingale/14876.article?adredir=1.

The Harrison Sisters' Trust. "The Harrison Sisters - Famous English Musicians." Accessed May 6, 2021. http://www.harrisonsisterstrust.org.uk/.

SPECIAL THANKS

With thanks to Patricia Cleveland-Peck and her meticulous editing of Beatrice Harrison's diary. —P.N.

Never-ending thank-yous to Margaret Quinlin, Jennifer Browne, and Vicky Holifield for trusting me with this wonderful project, for sharing their knowledge, and for letting me do what I so love to do.

And of course my biggest thank-you to Patricia Newman for writing Beatrice Harrison's brilliant, magical story. —I.F.

(top) Beatrice with her first cello at approximately age nine. Photo courtesy of Patricia Cleveland-Peck.

(bottom) Beatrice and one of her "star pupils" in 1923. Chronicle / Alamy